War Life

Sarah Fleming

Contents

The World at War

World War II began in 1939, when the German army invaded Poland. Countries all over the world joined the war. The war ended in 1945.

ALLIES		INVADING COUNTRIES		NEUTRAL COUNTRIES
United States	▢	Germany	▰	Switzerland, ▢
United Kingdom and colonies	▢	German occupied territory	▢	Spain, etc.
Australia	▰	Italy	▢	
Canada	▰	Japan	▰	
USSR	■	Japanese occupied territory	▰	
others	▰			

By 1940, Germany had invaded many European countries, and was trying to invade the United Kingdom.

Winston Churchill led Britain.

Winston Churchill

Adolf Hitler led Germany.

President Franklin Delano Roosevelt led the United States.

Adolf Hitler

Franklin D. Roosevelt

War Sources

How do we know what happened to people who lived in Europe during the war?

We have artifacts:

- letters
- **ration books**
- gas masks
- clothes
- photos.

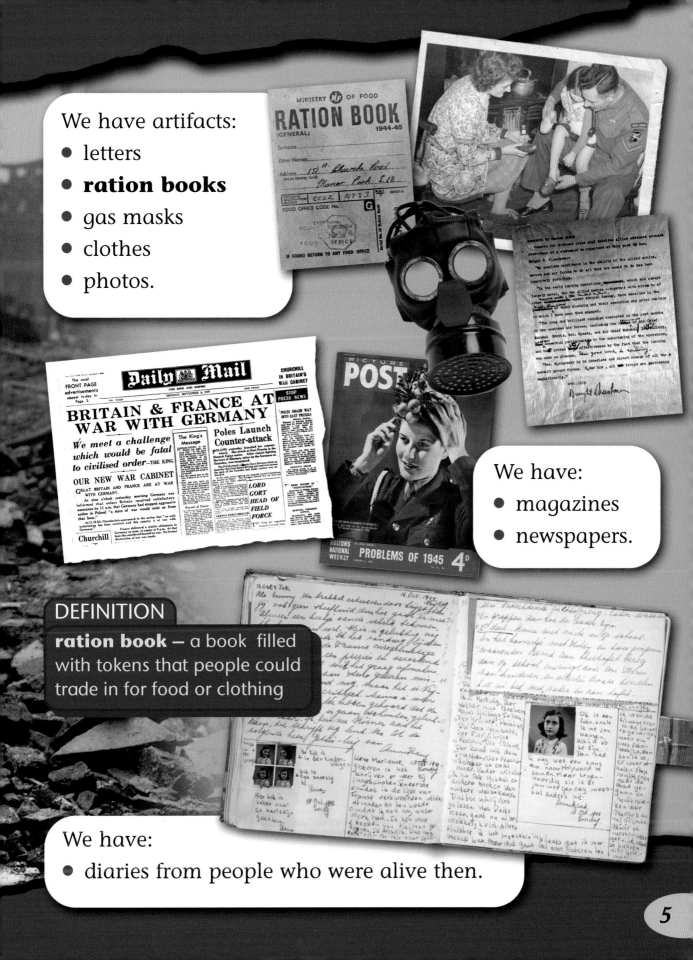

MINISTRY OF FOOD
RATION BOOK
(GENERAL)
1944-45

Surname:
Other Names:
Address:

We have:

- magazines
- newspapers.

Daily Mail

BRITAIN & FRANCE AT WAR WITH GERMANY

DEFINITION

ration book – a book filled with tokens that people could trade in for food or clothing

We have:

- diaries from people who were alive then.

A Child's War Memories

These are Jill's war memories. Jill was only seven when the war ended, so she doesn't remember everything that happened. Think about your early memories. Can you remember everything?

Jill age 7

Jill age 2

I was only two when the war started. I didn't know anything about living in peacetime, so being at war didn't seem strange.

UK

• Leicester

Norwich

Fordham

Ipswich

• Oxford

London

Dover

Brighton

Calais

Boulogne

Brugge

German Occupied France

Dieppe

Fécamp

Caen

Elbe Louvie

Key
East Anglia ▨

We lived in a town on the east coast of England called Fordham. Because it's flat and so near Germany, there were many **airfields** there. British **fighters** and **bombers** flew over us. German bombers flew over us too.

Bomb factory

Bombers

For a long time, bombers flew over almost every night. My brothers learned to tell the different noise each kind of airplane made. They could name all the airplanes, and they could tell which were British and which were German.

One night a bomb fell at the end of our driveway. It didn't explode, but we weren't allowed near it. The bomb was about four feet (120 cm) long, and gray. The army came to blow it up, and it made a big hole in the driveway.

The holes in this building were made when a bomb landed nearby.

Near the end of the war, the Germans sent **doodlebugs**. We would hear the **air raid** sirens and then listen for the doodlebugs – they made a loud whining noise. When the whining stopped, you knew that they were about to fall.

DEFINITION

doodlebugs – bombs with wings and an engine that were set off in Europe and flew over to Britain. They whistled as they flew, and then they were silent as they fell.

DEFINITION

air raid – an attack by aircraft

Gas Masks

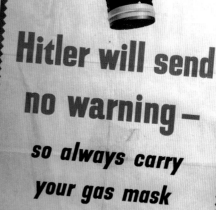

Hitler will send no warning – so always carry your gas mask

ISSUED BY THE MINISTRY OF HOME SECURITY

When the German planes attacked, we hid under the stairs. We took our **gas masks**. My parents and my brothers had black gas masks. Because I was little, I had one called a Mickey Mouse gas mask. It was red and blue.

Blackout

My father was an **air raid warden** for our town. Every night he went out on **blackout** patrol. He checked that no light was shining from any house.

Dogs wore bright coats to be seen in the blackout.

UNTIL YOUR EYES GET USED TO THE DARKNESS, TAKE IT EASY

LOOK OUT IN THE BLACKOUT

Air Raid

Once my mother and I took the train to London, England's capital. When we got there, we heard an air raid siren.

My mother took me down into an **underground station**. It was very crowded, hot, and stuffy. I remember my head jammed between people, seeing everyone's shoes, hundreds of shoes. I was glad when a siren rang to let us know that it was safe to come out.

In London, underground stations were used as air raid shelters.

Morrison shelter

Anderson shelter

DEFINITION
underground station — a station for the train system (called "the underground") that people use to travel in London

Food

Before World War II, countries bought and sold food to each other, sending it by ship. During the war, German warships and submarines bombed and sank many of these ships. In England, there wasn't much food.

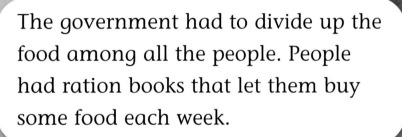

The government had to divide up the food among all the people. People had ration books that let them buy some food each week.

We each had our own jar for our sugar ration. When my mother made a cake, she took a spoonful of sugar out of each person's jar.

When people bought the food, the shopkeeper would cut out the ration coupons from the ration book.

We kept hens, pigs, and goats. My mother made butter with the goats' milk. When we killed a pig, she salted the meat and bottled it so it would not rot.

Parks and open land were dug up and used to grow vegetables to keep everyone fed.

There were recipe ideas in newspapers to make food more interesting.

My mother dried rings of apples to keep over the winter, and she bottled plums, and made lots of jam. There were no bananas, oranges, lemons, or grapes that made it to England during the war.

The only candy I had during the war were packages of **Horlicks tablets**. American soldiers gave them to me. The soldiers would come past in tanks and trucks as I walked to school.

DEFINITION

Horlicks tablets — small candy that tasted like malt

Clothes

Clothes were rationed too. You could not buy many new clothes. My mother made lots of my clothes from her old ones.

1942-43 CLOTHING BOOK

This book may not be used until the holder's name, full postal address and National Registration (Identity Card) Number have been plainly written below IN INK.

NAME
(BLOCK LETTERS)

ADDRESS 39 *Rectory Close*
(BLOCK LETTERS) *South Ruislip*

(TOWN)_____(COUNTY)

NATIONAL REGISTRATION (IDENTITY CARD) NUMBER

Read the instructions within carefully, and take great care not to lose this

To keep your shoes from wearing out, you put metal studs on the tip of the soles and the back of the heels.

MAKE-DO AND MEND

says Mrs. Sew-and-Sew

ISSUED BY THE BOARD OF TRADE

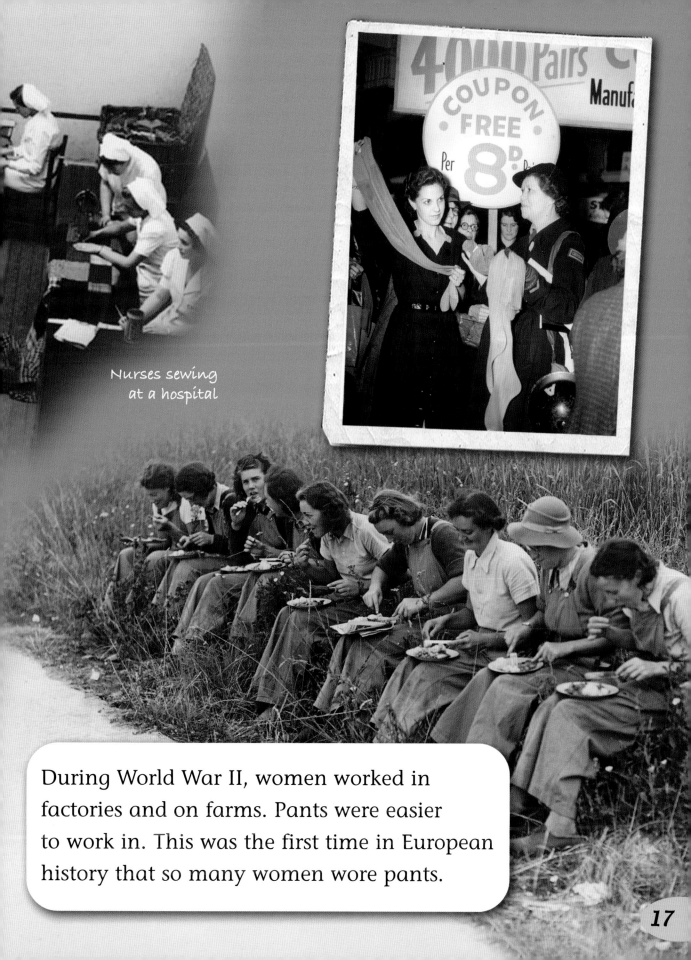

Nurses sewing
at a hospital

During World War II, women worked in factories and on farms. Pants were easier to work in. This was the first time in European history that so many women wore pants.

News

Every night my father would listen to the six o'clock news on his hissing radio.

Movie theaters showed news programs before the movies began.

Most people learned about the war from the radio and the newspapers. They didn't have televisions.

THE DAILY MAIL, Tuesday, December 31, 1940

More Of A Pal Than Ever

SHERLEY'S
TONIC AND CONDITION POWDERS

Daily Mail

FOR KING AND EMPIRE

NO. 13,941

TUESDAY, DECEMBER 31, 1940

ONE PENNY

Hitler Planned Monday Swoop

London was to Blaze First

By NOEL MONKS,
Daily Mail Air Correspondent

HITLER meant to start the second Great Fire of London as the prelude to an invasion.

This was the belief held in well-informed quarters in London yesterday.

The Nazis planned to set big fires burning all over London before midnight.

Relays of bombers laden with H.E. would then have carried out the most destructive raid of the war. The New Year invasion was to be followed.

The R.A.F. have given more details of the invasion ports in the past week than for two weeks or more. Clearly there is second reason for supposing that Hitler is still going ahead with invasion plans.

THE FACTS

We saw the real facts of Sunday night's fire-raising raid, as told to us yesterday.

Here is one of the biggest night raids on Britain since September.

R.A.F. night fighters were operating over the London area. High spots were doing so far as London and the coast, up to and after 10 p.m. the German Air Command sent out instructions for all its bombers engaged to return to their bases, as the weather had taken a turn for the worse and bad weather was coming out their aerodromes.

The weather, then, and not night fighters, that saved London an even worse attack. And it is held that the assault should have been the fiercest of the war.

1,000 bombers were to have used during the night. The objectives given for the second swoop of London's interior area—that is the light of one around which most of London and continue firing would need the positions of...

The German fighter's came down in lower numbers than ever before over London than ever they were able to do this...

The guns had stopped firing...

These lit up the barrage fire the raiders could fire here.

I noted that more than ordinary bombs were raining rapidly within three...

An hour last night no report from any...

Bad weather serious the experiments of the R.A.F.
Sunday night had to be...

All Sees n's Ruins

CHURCHILL, accompanied by his wife, visited St. Paul's Churchyard and spent two hours visiting...

and should, "God bless Churchill" as...

"Keep under..."

"A minute of the crowd. "Good luck to..."

...obeying a woman at churchyard. "When she asked: turned to... when we're...

Even as a...

WAR'S GREATEST PICTURE: St. Paul's Stands Unharmed in the Midst of the Burning City

ROAR of gun barrage mingled with roar and crackle of flames raiders droned overhead. Daily Mail cameraman H. A. Mason stood on a City roof to get this awe-inspiring picture of the second Great Fire of London—St. Paul's Cathedral ringed with flame. "I focussed at intervals as the great dome loomed up through the smoke," he said. "Glare of many fires and sweeping clouds of smoke kept hiding the shape. Then a wind sprang up. Suddenly the shining cross, dome and towers stood out like a symbol in an inferno. The scene was unbelievable. In that moment or two I released my shutter. Here is my picture, one that all Britain will cherish—for it symbolises the steadiness of London's stand against the enemy—the firmness of Right against Wrong." Other pictures showing the raid havoc are in the BACK Pages.

HAVOC COULD HAVE BEEN SAVED

By Daily Mail Reporter

MANY of Sunday night's fires in the City of London could have been avoided if fire-watching regulations had been properly observed.

That is the opinion of Commander A. N. G. Firebrace, the London Fire Brigade chief, who has just transferred to the Home Office to help in organising local fire brigade duties through the country.

"I should be a point of fire," he declared, "a point of fire. If you have fire-watching, if you will not be in your place burn down both for my own make and for the sake of my neighbours."

Fire-fighting experts said about the same thing about the absence of fire-watching staff that had been on duty at all the fires affecting any at all the fires would have been prevented.

What happened is now a little fire start, and then to burn an hour to see the whole roof ablaze.

What happened is not merely ponderous described it as "a mass attack concentrated in the space of a few hours, caused a relatively small space, said, a relatively strong force name as a strong force mass a name as a German side of the situation...

Employed at the various fires almost every form of fire used to ensure min on Sunday...

Berlin Radio Went 'All Quiet'

Berlin radio eliminated all reference to the destruction of its broadcast account last night of the fire raid on London. Neither did it follow its usual practice of giving interviews with raiding pilots.

Bremen Radio's English announcer described it as "a fierce mass attack concentrated in the space of a few hours.

"A great number of fires were caused in a relatively small space," said, "within the attack was waged a name as a strong force..."

The New York Sun: "Deadly implacable insists towards the dictatorships scuttled every phase."

New York Post: One of the major declarations of the six First 5...

100 to 1 Backing for Roosevelt

From Daily Mail Correspondent

WASHINGTON, Monday.

PRESIDENT ROOSEVELT is "tremendously pleased" at the reaction to his speech, in which he pledged more aid to Britain and declared that the Axis could not win the war.

The President's secretary, Mr. Stephen Early, said to-day that the address had brought a greater response than any previous Roosevelt talk.

Within 40 minutes of its end the President received 600 messages. They were 100 to 1 in favour.

This is how it was received by Senator Allen Barkley, leader of the Democratic Party in the Senate—its emphasised clarification of our objectives.

Senator Warren R. Austin, leader of Republican Party Minority in the Senate, remarkably the presentation, for the situation.

Some of the pinnacst American strategists favour the transfer of at least 400 of the latest type purchase and bomber planes, as six First 5...

China Seeks U.S. Planes

From Daily Mail Correspondent

NEW YORK, Monday.—The United States Government are posted to be considering the release of its warplanes to China for use against the Japanese.

Major-General Sun-chu Mow head of the Chinese Air Force, is Washington conferring with Administration officials and Army and Navy leaders.

America Moves

BIG ARMS FLOW HAS BEGUN

From Daily Mail Correspondent

NEW YORK, Monday.

THE United States Defence Commission announced to-day that they had approved arms contracts worth £1,500,000,000.

Monthly production had now risen to 2,400 aircraft engines, 700 warplanes, 100 tanks, and 10,000 automatic rifles.

Present British and American orders on hand total: 50,000 planes, 130,000 aero-engines, 8,200 tanks, 2,035,000 guns, 380 naval vessels, 200 merchant ships, 50,000 lorries, and other equipment.

The United States Government were building 40 war factories, including the first plant for mass-producing tanks.

LATEST

MORE U.S. AID FOR GREECE

WASHINGTON, Monday.
Mr. Morgenthau, Secretary of the Treasury, indicated to-day that President Roosevelt may extend his loan or lease plan to Greece and China, in addition to Britain.—Exchange.

ADMIRAL LEAHY REACHES EUROPE

VICHY, Monday.—Admiral Leahy, the new American Ambassador to the French Government at Vichy, has arrived in Lisbon on board the United States cruiser Tuscaloosa, states a Havas despatch.—Reuter.

LONDON LULLABY

Meet Richard: An Eyewitness's Account

Look at the main story in the newspaper on the last page. Richard Fleming saw the fire.

Lance Corporal Richard Fleming

In 1940, I was in the part of the army that had to catch spies.

I could speak German. My job was to go into restaurants in London and listen to anyone speaking German. I was trying to catch spies. Of course, I never found any!

My **headquarters** were on a hill from where you could see most of London.

The center part of London is called The City, and it is where London began. It has a lot of old buildings, including the Tower of London and many banks.

In the winter of 1940, London was bombed night after night. One evening in December, the sky over the city glowed red. There must have been a huge air raid. My boss decided to go and see what was going on, and I asked if I could go with him.

In the Blazing City

We went in a little army van with a canvas roof. When we got near St. Paul's Cathedral, we saw that all the buildings around it were on fire, but luckily not the cathedral itself. There was lots of smoke, and pieces of burning building falling onto the streets.

There were huge clouds of burning cinders blowing down the streets, and we realized it was no place to be sightseeing in a van with a canvas roof!

Firemen were trying to stop the blaze. Hundreds of fire hoses were stretched out over the streets. I remember the mushy feeling as we drove over them.

At one point, a policeman came up to us and said, "I wouldn't go near those buildings if I were you, sir. Great burning lumps are falling off all the time. Stay near the cathedral." I think because we were in uniform he thought we were there on important business. We got back to headquarters as quickly as we could!

After the Raid

the day after

Many buildings around St. Paul's Cathedral were bombed during the war. If you go to that area today, you will see many new ones that were built in their place.